W9-BZB-120

DATE DUE			

AUG - - 2018

Pigs

Julie Murray

Abdo
FARM ANIMALS
Kids

Children's
636.4
Murray

abdopublishing.com

Published by Abdo Kids, a division of ABDO, PO Box 398166, Minneapolis, Minnesota 55439.
Copyright © 2016 by Abdo Consulting Group, Inc. International copyrights reserved in all countries.
No part of this book may be reproduced in any form without written permission from the publisher.

Printed in the United States of America, North Mankato, Minnesota.

052015

092015

THIS BOOK CONTAINS
RECYCLED MATERIALS

Photo Credits: iStock, Shutterstock

Production Contributors: Teddy Borth, Jennie Forsberg, Grace Hansen

Design Contributors: Candice Keimig, Dorothy Toth

Library of Congress Control Number: 2014960327

Cataloging-in-Publication Data

Murray, Julie.

 Pigs / Julie Murray.

   p. cm. -- (Farm animals)

ISBN 978-1-62970-942-0

Includes index.

1. Swine--Juvenile literature.   I. Title.

636.4--dc23

                    2014960327

Table of Contents

Pigs

Pigs live on farms.

Some pigs are pink or brown.

Others are black.

Some have spots or **markings**.

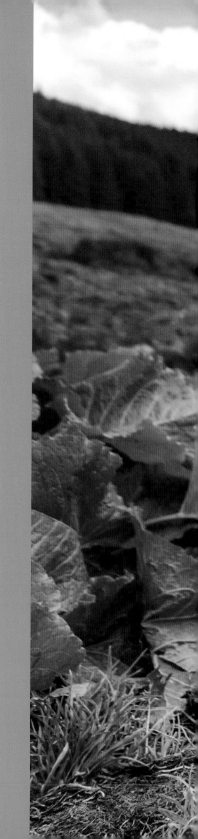

A pig's nose is called a snout. Pigs have a good sense of smell!

Girl pigs are called sows.

Boys are boars.

Babies are piglets.

sow

boar

piglet

11

Pigs say, "oink."

13

Pigs roll in the mud.

This keeps them cool.

Pigs eat **grain**.

They also eat **roots** and fruit.

Meat from a pig is called pork.

Do you like ham or bacon?

They come from pigs!

Have you seen pigs on a farm?

A Pig's Life

drink water

have fun in the mud

eat

rest

Glossary

grain
the seeds of plants that are used for food.

marking
a mark or repeated mark on an animal's fur or skin.

root
the part of a plant that grows underground. It gives water and nutrients to the plant.

Index

abdokids.com

Use this code to log on to abdokids.com and access crafts, games, videos, and more!

Abdo Kids Code:
FPK9420

24